The Daily Show's
Five Questions
from
Comedy Central

The Daily Show's
Five Questions
from
Comedy Central

Introduction by Craig Kilborn

Andrews McMeel
Publishing
Kansas City

www.andrewsmcmeel.com

98 99 00 01 02 BAH 10 9 8 7 6 5 4 3 2 1

The Daily Show's five questions from Comedy Central / introduction by Craig Kilborn.
    p. cm.
    ISBN 0-8362-5325-6 (pbk.)
    1. American wit and humor.   I. Daily Show II. Comedy Central
(Performing group)
PN6162.D26   1998
791.45'72--dc21

                                 97-48737
                                      CIP

Book designed by Blair Graphic Design
Cover designed by Comedy Central
Cover photo by Frank Veronsky

ATTENTION: SCHOOLS AND BUSINESSES

Andrews McMeel books are available at quantity discounts with bulk purchase for educational, business, or sales promotional use. For information, please write to: Special Sales Department, Andrews McMeel Publishing, 4520 Main Street, Kansas City, Missouri 64111.

FOREWORD
by Craig Kilborn

Lots of questions—"Hey, Craiggers, the Five Questions thing, how did it all happen?"

Good question. You kids are really starting to think out there.

Not a short answer, however. It's more of what we'd call a multi-leveled response. There are layers here. Many different layers. Layers you have to peel back. Like on an onion. An onion that stinks and maybe even makes you cry but when you sauté it in a little olive oil with  some garlic and tomatoes and spices and spread it over pasta cooked al dente, it can also make you a little bit happy. That's kind of what we're dealing with here. Let's call it an emotional roller-coaster ride. Brace yourselves.

Looking back, I can almost smile about it now. Almost—but not quite.

The escape was pretty clean. And it was long over-due. Hey, I put in my time! Just how long does a man have to put up with hellish conditions like that? The scratching, the spitting, the satellite dishes. It was primitive, demeaning, animalistic. It reached down your throat and ripped out your insides. All the while just laughing at you. The laughter bouncing off the bleeding walls of an empty, cavernous torso. It was an existence—almost a nonexistence, really—propelled by demonic machinations designed to make you feel insignificant, unworthy, unclean. It was just not right. Not right at all.

But ESPN and Bristol, Connecticut—and all that they represent—were now just memories. Distant mem-ories. Fading memories. Really bad memories.

But what the hell, it was a gig—and I still had my looks, which were really important to me. And I was finally in a good place. I was just weeks away from a new start in a new town. *The Daily Show.* Comedy Central. A real network with real people doing a real job. No more sports—that stuff of youth. The kind of stuff that retards your growth as an adult. The kind of stuff that mires you in a cesspool of dysfunction. No. This was "The News." The front of the paper. Important stuff. I love important stuff.

But that's not important right now.

It was a Sunday night in June. The kind of night other people would call balmy but I would never say that because I hate the word balmy. So, anyway, it was, well, sort of a thick night in June and I was a little tired. I was also a little curious about what was out there in this, my new town, the city that never sleeps, the Apple. I was ready for a bite, and someone—and it really doesn't matter who—suggested a cocktail at the Bowery Bar.

I had never been to the Bowery Bar before, but I had been known to enjoy a cocktail on occasion—so this was that exhilarating mix of the known and the unknown. This was the fun part.

I left the house and I was still a little tired. I was dressed in khaki pants, a white T-shirt, a gray pullover sweater, blond hair, and blue eyes. They look good on me. I took a cab downtown. I tipped the driver 20 percent. I'm just that big of a guy.

I walked into the bar, and I saw her almost immediately. Very pretty. Very sophisticated. Just so, very. She looked like a young Natalie Wood. I said this to myself. I also said it to her a little bit later. Hey, why not? It was a good line, and I was still a little tired. She responded that people would often tell her mother that she (her mother, not the girl in front of me at the bar) looked like Natalie Wood. So far, so good. Maybe I even had a shot with her mother. This was the really fun part.

We started to talk the way people do at first—tentatively, cautiously, flirtatiously. We found that we had so much in common. She looked like a young Natalie Wood, and I looked like a young me. She was at the Bowery Bar, and I was there, too. What's more, I was a little tired and so was she. This was, as we say in the business, fate, kismet, the Champs D'Elysee.

Have I mentioned that I'm a little tired at this point? That's important to know because I didn't want to waste any time. I wanted to—no, I had to—cut to the chase.

Then it came to me, as all ideas do, BOOM! Like an epiphany or something like that. I'll reduce the conversation to five questions. Make it a game. I love games. I grew up playing Password and Trivial Pursuit, and I think people should know the capitals of every state in the Union. That's the kind of stuff that's important to me.

She perked right up. I guess she liked games, too.

The first question—very important. "What do you think about garlic?"

Now, garlic is one of those things that you either love or hate. There's no middle ground here. You can't say, "Well, it's okay"—because that's just not okay. When it comes to garlic you have to have passion. I happen to love the stuff—passionately.

And her? Well, she loved it, too. This was going well.

Question two. "Have you ever been to Carmel, California?"

Carmel is also important to me. I lived there for a while and I loved it. Clint Eastwood was the mayor, and the streets were clean and safe and everyone prospered. Carmel, for me, is the Utopian ideal. I will retire there someday. I know that now—and I knew that then.

And her? YES! Not only had she visited that delightful little hamlet, her grandmother used to have a place there. She found it quite appealing. This was going very well.

Question three. At this point, you should know that I have a brother who is very bright—the sole valedictorian of his high school graduating class of 500 (not the year, the number of students). I like having a smart brother—and I would often show him off.

Once, a friend of mine tested my brother's vocabulary by asking, "What does 'peripatetic' mean?" My brother said "itinerant." My brother was right. Like I said, he is very bright.

So, question three for the young Natalie Wood look-alike. "What does 'peripatetic' mean?"

I noticed a visible frown—as frowns are usually visible. Now, I knew what peripatetic means because my brother, who is very bright, told me. And her? Her response was short, terse, not so sweet. "What the hell kind of a question is that?"

Things were not going very well anymore. But things like that happen. No need to dwell, linger, ruminate. Time to move on, advance, push ahead.

Like I said, an emotional roller-coaster ride. And so what if the very first Five Questions were really just three questions in length? And maybe I didn't get the girl, but that's not what is important to me.

I did get a great segment for the show. And I got to use peripatetic for two weeks before Gordon Elliot came up with the proper definition. Let's face it, when everything is all said and done, that is what's really important to me.

Good question, everybody! Now let's go right over to the next page.

Bill Murray

(score: 5/5)

Q. *What is the capital of Finland?*
A. "Helsinki. But can I name a second city in
Finland? No!"
Correct!

Q. *Name a '70s Bulls white center.*
A. "Tommy Berwinkle."
Correct!

Q. *Who do you find more attractive: Greta Van
Susteren or Joanne Worley?*
A. "I'm going to go with Greta . . . Who is Greta?"
Correct!

Who left the cake out in the rain?

Q. *Use the word "whack" in a sentence.*
A. "The drill sergeant gave the private a whack."
   Correct!

Q. *Who left the cake out in the rain?*
A. "Someone."
   Correct!

Chevy Chase

(score: 2/5)

Q. *Before they moved to Los Angeles, where did the Lakers play?*

A. "Oh, that's an easy one, Bob. Burundi. Oh, I'm sorry. Milwaukee."
Incorrect! It's Minneapolis.

Q. *Which elves make cookies in hollow trees?*

A. "The Osmonds."
Incorrect! The Keebler elves.

Q. *Who was the thirty-eighth president of the United States of America?*

A. "We've had that many? Uh, Jackson, uh, Jackson . . . Jesse—uh . . ."
Incorrect! Gerald Ford.

Q. *Besides* She's Gotta Have It, *name your favorite Spike Lee movie.*

A. "Uh, was he on the Lakers?" *Correct! We're gonna take that, 'cause it's hard to name those.*

Q. *Do you ever get the urge late at night to put on a red teddy with a ski mask, get in the car, and drive around and just crank Loverboy?*

A. "Not only do I get the urge, but every ten minutes. So I go put that stuff on, go to the bathroom . . ." *Correct!*

Which elves make cookies in hollow trees?

John Cleese

(score: 5/5)

Q. *What is the capital of Belgium?*
A. "Brussels."
Correct!

Q. *Define "ipso facto."*
A. "In and of itself."
Correct!

Q. *Name your favorite Charlie's Angel.*
A. "Noam Chomsky."
Uh, correct!

Name your favorite Charlie's Angel.

Q. *True or false: The Irish are all drunks.*
A. (Long pause) "Talse. No, frue, frue!"
Correct! False, we shouldn't fall prey to cultural stereotypes.

Q. *Why does British food suck?*
A. "We had an empire to run!"
Correct!

Mark Curry

(score: 2/5)

Q. *Which is the Hoosier State?*
A. "Indiana, baby! Bobby Knight, Bobby Knight!"
Correct!

Q. *What duo was a little bit country, a little bit rock 'n' roll?*
A. "Snoop Doggy Dogg and Dr. Dre!"
Incorrect! Donny and Marie.

Q. *What's the difference between a boil and a blister?*
A. "One you have to go to the doctor quicker."
Incorrect! A boil is a pus-filled swelling of the skin, a blister is a fluid-filled skin eruption.

Q. *Who's the best forward ever?*
A. "Ladies and gentlemen, let's give it up for Elvin Hayes."
Incorrect! Larry Bird.

Q. *How high is the sky?*
A. "It depends on what you're smoking."
Correct!

What's the difference between a boil and a blister?

Michael J. Fox

(score 4/5)

Q. *Name three Canadian provinces that begin with the letter "N."*
A. "Newfoundland, New Brunswick, and Nova Scotia."
Right!

Q. *True or False: You once dated Susan Anton.*
A. "I once went up on Susan Anton."
We're gonna take that, yes!

Q. *Who was the last NHL goalie to play without a mask?*
A. "Gump Worsley."
Yes!

The Daily Show's Five Questions

Family Ties :
Skippy,
dufus or dork?

Q. Family Ties: *Skippy, dufus or dork?*
A. "I want to say dorkus. I have to go for dork."
   No, Dufus.

Q. *Finally, size: Does it matter?*
A. "Yes, absolutely."
   Yes!

Janeane Garofalo

(score: 4/5)

Q. *Where is the J. Paul Getty Museum?*
A. "Los Angeles, California."
Correct!

Q. *Who wrote the neoclassic* Mountain, Get Out of My Way?
A. "Mohammed."
Incorrect! Montel Williams.

Q. *Point to your proboscis.*
A. (Janeane points to her nose)
Correct!

Why can't you smile and just be happy all the time?

Q. *What makes better chocolate milk, Nestlés Quik or Hershey's syrup?*
A. "Nestlés Quik."
Correct!

Q. *Why can't you smile and just be happy all the time?*
A. "Um . . . because of all the tragedy in the world?"
Correct!

Mike Myers

(score: 4/5)

Q. *What are people from Liverpool called?*
A. "Liverpudlians."
Correct!

Q. *Name the ingredients in shepherd's pie.*
A. "Uh, mashed potatoes, uh, minced beef, pearl onions, carrots."
Correct!

Q. *Worst Bond movie song: Carly Simon's "Nobody Does It Better" or Sheena Easton's "For Your Eyes Only"?*
A. "'For Your Eyes Only.'"
Incorrect! No, we're gonna say the other one—ever since "Sugar Walls" I've loved Sheena Easton.

Canada: What went wrong?

Q. *More fun to say: Esa Tikkanen or Joe Juneau?*
A. "Esa Tikkanen."
Correct!

Q. *Canada: What went wrong?*
A. "I remember a little thing called the War of 1812. I believe we kicked some Yankee butt."
Correct! We're gonna give that to you.

John Tesh
(score 5/5)

Q. *What is Sequoia National Park famous for?*
A. "Redwoods."
Correct!

Q. *With the exception of the actual potatoes, what is the other main ingredient in classic American potato salad?*
A. "Mayonnaise."
Correct!

Q. *Use the word "skanky" in a sentence.*
A. "When I'm near you, I feel skanky."
I guess so, correct.

Q. *Would you rather take a swing at Michael Bolton or Yanni?*

A. "Michael Bolton."
Correct!

Q. *Finally, are you and your wife still celibate or do you occasionally get it on?*

A. "We are regular."
Correct!

Use the word "skanky" in a sentence.

French Stewart

(score 2/5)

Q. *What is known as the second planet from the sun?*
A. "Would that be Mercury?"
No, Venus.

Q. *What are European french fry condiments?*
A. "Gouda?"
No. We're looking for mayo or mustard.

Q. *John Lithgow wore a dress in what Robin Williams movie?*
A. "It was not *Buckaroo Bonzai*."
Oh, you're 0 for 3, Garp.

John Lithgow wore a dress in what Robin Williams movie?

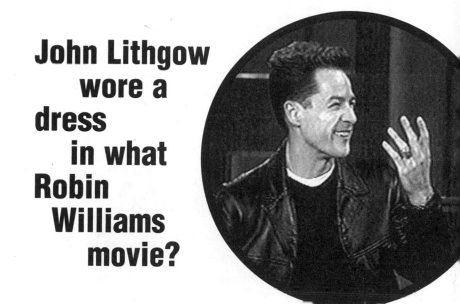

Q. *Who was Buffy and Jody's governess?*
A. "French."
Yes!

Q. *Live up to your name and say something in French.*
A. "Oui."
Yes!

Charo
(score: 4/5)

Q. *What state is Boston in?*
A. "Oh, come on, everybody know that, even my chi-huahua. Machachushet (Massachusetts)."
Correct!

Q. *How do you make a corn dog?*
A. "Corn, C-O-R-N? The thin' tha' chu eat? How you make it, a corn dog? Oh, chure. You stig it with sugar, caramello, and then you . . ."
Incorrect! No, I'm sorry. Corn meal on a hot dog, then deep-fried.

Q. *Who looks better in a white suit: Gavin MacLeod or Ricardo Montalban?*

A. "Well listen, I like both. I have to choose one? Because they both are very cute. Okay, okay, Ricardo Montalban."
Correct!

Q. *What makes a Blue Hawaiian blue?*

A. "Tha blue thin'."
Correct. The blue thing. Yeah. I don't care.

Q. *Do you dream in English or Spanish?*

A. "Oh jess, oh, wait a minute, I dream in English. 'Money, money, money, money . . .'"
Correct! We're gonna give that to you.

How do you make a corn dog?

Richard Lewis

(score: 4/5)

Q. *What's the capital of Florida?*
A. "Tallahassee."
Correct!

Q. *With the exception of the Renaissance, name your favorite historical period.*
A. "The period where no one got yeast infections."
Correct!

Q. *Use the phrase "paranoid schizophrenic" in a sentence.*
A. "Hi, how are you?"
Correct!

With the exception of the Renaissance, name your favorite historical period.

Q. *Name your favorite Lou Rawls song.*
A. "Ah, you know, 'Hi, There's a Bush.'"
Incorrect! "You'll Never Find."

Q. *Would you like fries with that?*
A. "Huh? What's the question? . . . Oh. No friggin' way!"
Correct!

Michael Palin

(score 3/5)

Q. *What is the creatively named desert in western Australia?*
A. "The Simpson Desert."
Incorrect.

Q. *What is "grappa"?*
A. "An Italian drink made from grape stalks."
Correct!

Q. *Name the annoying Redgrave.*
A. "Vanessa."
Correct!

Q. *What's the air speed velocity of an unladen swallow?*
A. "Three months, two days and one hour."
Incorrect.

Q. *Why can't you just call it soccer, like we do?*
A. "Because we have a Football Association and it has a flag."
Correct!

Why can't you just call it soccer, like we do?

from Comedy Central

Dyan Cannon

(score: 3/5)

Q. *What is the birthplace of grunge?*
A. "Seattle."
Correct!

Q. *Name the only team in the '80s who got swept twice in the NBA finals.*
A. "Peanut Butter."
Incorrect! We would have accepted Lakers.
"AAAhhhh, they told me that the answer to the second question was 'peanut butter.' They lied, they lied . . . They said they wanted me to be the first person on the show to get five right."

Q. *Finish this lyric: "What the world needs now, is . . ."*
A. "Peanut butter, no—'love sweet love.'"
Correct!

Finish this lyric: "What the world needs now, is . . ."

Q. *More inspiring TV:* Touched by an Angel *or* Dr. Quinn, Medicine Woman*?*
A. *"Touched by an Angel."*
Correct!

Q. *Do you find this irritating?*
A. *"'Yes. Brian, you are so attractive.'"*
"It's Craig! Time out! She just did the Letterman show with Brian Williams the anchor and she keeps calling me Brian. That's kind of funny, isn't it? Let's have a big hand for Farrah Fawcett Majors."

Joan Rivers

(score: 3/5)

Q. *What's the Beaver State?*
A. *"Rhode Island."*
   Incorrect! Oregon.

Q. *What's in guacamole?*
A. *"Avocado."*
   Correct!

Where do babies come from?

Q. *Who's more attractive, Fabio or a young Robert Wagner?*
A. "Fabio."
Incorrect! A young Robert Wagner.

Q. *Where do babies come from?*
A. "I don't know, but I have three eggs in my refrigerator."
Correct!

Q. *Favorite Madonna song?*
A. "'Who's the Daddy.'"
Correct!

Peter Fonda

(score: 4/5)

Q. *Where is Fond Du Lac?*
A. "New York."
Incorrect! Wisconsin.

Q. *Who is the female lead of TV's* Suddenly Susan?
A. "Brooke Shields."
Correct!

Q. *Finish this lyric: "War, good God y'all . . ."*
A. "What is it good for."
Correct!

Does Bridget ever ask about me?

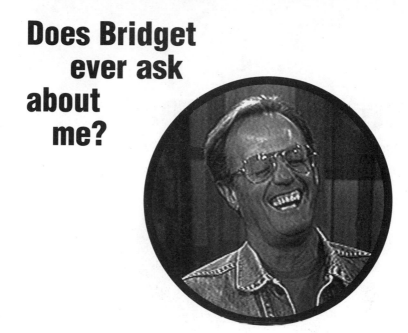

Q. *What is the title of Jack Kerouac's seminal work?*
A. "On the Road."
Correct!

Q. *Does Bridget ever ask about me?*
A. "As a matter of fact, you're not going to believe this, she doesn't ask a word about you."
Correct!

Brenda Vaccaro

(score: 3/5)

Q. *What's the capital of Connecticut?*
A. "Westport."
Incorrect! Hartford.

Q. *What was Gofer's job on* The Love Boat?
A. "Gofer's job—you know what he did all over the boat, he was goofing and gofing and he was doing all these things that only gophers know how to do, so there were a lot of holes on the boat . . ."
Correct! Or purser.

Q. *Finish this sentence: Plop, plop, fizz, fizz.*
A. "Oh, my God, you'll have the best B.M. you ever had."
Correct!

Tampon
or
pad?

Q. *Name the ingredients of tiramisu.*

A. "Oh, my God, that's why you need the plop, plop, fizz, fizz, because it has cream chocolate, pastry— this is the most embarrassing kind of colon exercise I've ever had!"

Incorrect! Ladyfingers, espresso coffee.

Q. *Tampon or pad?*

A. "I didn't do any hygiene [commercials]; my name is Melissa Jonesby, and I've never done a commercial in my life!"

Correct!

Kevin Meaney

(score: 4/5)

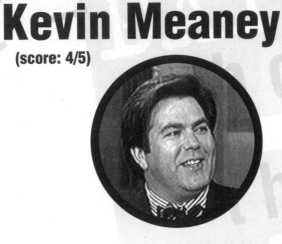

Q. *What is the nickname of San Francisco?*
A. "Uh . . . uh . . . disco. Frisco!"
Incorrect! No, they hate that. The City.

Q. *Name the original kids in "My Three Sons."*
A. "Ernie . . . "
Ernie was adopted . . .
"All right, he was adopted!
Bobby . . . and . . .
Bobby. Bob. Rob. Rob
and Chip. And Eddie."
And Mike.
"Mike!"
Correct!

What is a sneeze guard?

Q. *Use the word "unctuous" in a sentence.*
A. "Unctuous . . . I was walking down the street the other day and . . . and this 'unctuous' . . . professor . . . demanded my . . . tie!"
Correct! We have to accept that.

Q. *What is a sneeze guard?*
A. "That's over a salad bar."
Correct!

Q. *Have you never been mellow?*
A. "I've never been me- . . . well, I have been . . . no, I've never been mellow."
Have you never tried?
"I've never tried."
Correct! We're gonna accept that.

Jaleel White

(score 3/5)

Q. *What's the school nickname for Pepperdine University?*
A. *"The Waves."*
Correct!

Q. *What makes a dry martini dry?*
A. *"An olive."*
Incorrect.

Q. *Who's got better hops: "Webster" or Gary Coleman?*
A. *"Conrad Bain."*
Correct!

Q. *What child star said, "Let's put on a show"?*
A. *"Ron Howard." Incorrect.*

Q. *Rough estimate, when will you be entering puberty?*
A. *(Throws water on Craig.) Correct!*

Who's got better hops: "Webster" or Gary Coleman?

Elayne Boosler

(score: 4/5)

Q. *Name the Beehive State.*
A. "The Beehive State—that would be California in the '50s, I believe."
Incorrect! Or . . . Utah. We can't accept that. Very close, though.

Q. *Are birds mammals?*
A. "Uh, only after some horrible flying over Three Mile Island, perhaps they become mammals."
Correct! Right, they're not. They have their own phylum.

Q. *Finish this lyric: "No parking, baby . . ."*
A. "Oh! that's my favorite song on earth. 'No parking on the dance floor, baby.'"
Correct!

Which household product has "scrubbing bubbles"?

Q. *Which household product has "scrubbing bubbles"?*
A. "That would be Massengill, I believe."
Correct! Yes, I think we're accepting that.

Q. *How would I look in a tanktop?*
A. "Every man in a tanktop looks like my Aunt Sophie; don't do it."
Correct!

Wilt Chamberlain

(score: 4/5)

Q. *What are the three races in the Triple Crown?*
A. "One's Pembroke, the Kentucky Derby, and uh . . .
let's see, uh . . ."
Did you say Preakness?
"Preakness."
Did you say Belmont Stakes?
"Belmont Stakes."
Correct!

Q. *Who sang "Pull Up to the Bumper"?*
A. "The Orioles."
Remember, you worked on a movie with her.
"Oh, yeah, Grace Jones."
Correct!

Who sang "Pull Up to the Bumper"?

Q. *Will Shaquille O'Neal ever be as good as you?*
A. "He already is!"
No.
"With the movies, and the singing . . ."
Incorrect!

Q. *The category is cheese. What's more fun to say: Gouda or Havarti?*
A. "Havarti."
Correct!

Q. *Of your 20,000 women, how many did you cuddle with afterward?*
A. "At one time?"
No, afterward. How many did you hold?
"I'm still holding. I'm in a holding pattern."
Correct!

Christopher Guest

(score: 4/5)

Q. *What is the San Francisco treat?*
A. "You want the real answer? It's Rice-a-Roni."
Correct!

Q. *Name Fred Willard's character . . ."*
A. "Jerry . . . Yes."
Correct!

Q. *What is the first album Christopher Guest ever owned?*
A. "Hmm, first album I've ever . . . Hey, how do you know the answer to this?"
Incorrect! You won't get it, I don't think, because the answer is The Best of the Stylistics, *Craig's first album.*

What is the San Francisco treat?

Q. *Finish this sentence: "I hate it when . . ."*
A. "Yes. Oh, I see, I have to finish that. I hate when that happens. It's a bit I used to do on *Saturday Night Live* with Billy Crystal. Thank you."
Correct!

Q. *Skim milk, 2 percent, or whole?*
A. "Harold Doda. Okay, 2 percent."
Correct!

Keith Olbermann
(score: 3/5)

Q. *What is the most godforsaken place on the East Coast?*
A. "Bristol, Connecticut."
Correct!

Q. *More attractive: the Fabulous Sports Babe or Gordie Howe?*
A. "Gordie Howe."
Correct! Looking for Mr. Hockey, yes.

Q. *Name your favorite two sides at Boston Market.*
A. "Uh . . . oh! let's see, I love the corn bread, and also the uh . . . the uh . . . green stuff with the . . . "
The spinach?
"The spinach."
Incorrect! No, mashed potatoes, macaroni and cheese. Gotta carbo-load.

What is the most godforsaken place on the East Coast?

Q. *In 1961 Roger Maris led the majors in home runs. That year, who got hit in the head with the most balls?*
A. "Got hit in the head with . . . uh . . . "
Incorrect! Liberace.

Q. *Do you miss me?*
A. "Oh, intensely so."
Correct!

Jon Stewart

(score: 2/5)

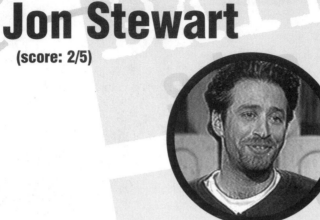

Q. *What is the capital of Kentucky?*
A. "Lexington."
Incorrect! Frankfort.

Q. *Finish this Barry White lyric: "Your sweetness is my . . ."*
A. ". . . feetness."
Incorrect! Weakness.

Q. *Favorite McDonald's entree?*
A. "Big Mac, #1, Super Size!"
Incorrect! Fillet o' Fish.

Q. *Name the three* Happy Days *spinoffs.*

A. *"Joanie Loves Chachi, Pottsie Takes It in the Ass, and ER."*
Correct! Mork and Mindy, Laverne & Shirley, *and* Joanie Loves Chachi.

Q. *What does "sorg dich nicht" mean?*

A. "It means, 'Germans will put you in camps and take your money.'"
Correct! Or, not to worry.

Finish this Barry White lyric: "Your sweetness is my . . ."

Tisha Campbell
(score: 5/5)

Q. *Which state is lovingly referred to as the "Armpit of New York"?*
A. "New Jersey."
Correct!

Q. *More absorbent paper towel: Bounty or Viva?*
A. "Bounty."
Correct! Yes, it's the quicker picker-upper.

Q. *Use the hipster slang "neato" in a sentence.*
A. "I really like being on this show, it's really 'neato.'"
Correct!

More absorbent paper towel: Bounty or Viva?

Q. *Finish this Carpenters song lyric: "Why do birds suddenly appear . . ."*
A. ". . . every time you are near.'"
Correct!

Q. *What's the recipe for a Craiggers Kilborn?*
A. "Um, two parts neato, and one part . . . uh . . . Ron Howard?"
Correct!

Sammy Hagar

(score: 3/5)

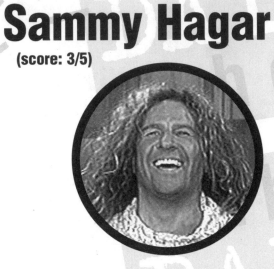

Q. *Where in the United States is the replica of the Parthenon?*
A. "That's in South Dakota."
Incorrect! I don't think we can accept that, because it's actually Nashville.

Q. *What are the most comfortable slacks you can buy?*
A. "Haggar slacks, absolutely."
Correct!

Q. *Worst hair: Gene Simmons or Gene Shalit?*
A. "I dunno, I gotta go with Gene Simmons, that's some bad hair."
Correct! Shalit's hair is natural and real.

What are the most comfortable slacks you can buy?

Q. *Name the ingredients of a Harvey Wullbanger.*

A. "Oh. You take fresh lime juice, squeeze it into, uh, over ice, double that with Cointreau, double that with tequila, shake it, pour it into a salt-rimmed glass."
Incorrect! Screwdriver with a shot of Galliano.

Q. *Who's the blond woman who ruined Van Halen?*

A. "David Lee Roth?"
Correct!

Kathy Ireland

(score: 1/5)

Q. *What is the "Show Me" State?*
A. (No response.)
Incorrect! It's Missouri.

Q. *Name three varieties of melon.*
A. "Canteloupe, honeydew, and watermelon."
Correct!

Q. *Tommy Lee or Gene Simmons?*
A. "Tommy Lee or Gene Simmons what?"
Incorrect!

Q. *Finish this lyric: "Reunited and . . ."*
A. *"Can you hum a bar?"*
Incorrect! ". . . and it feels so good."

Q. *What three words best describe you?*
A. *"Um, um, um . . . "*
We'll take it!*

*The judges were forced to reconsider, and it was determined they could not, in good conscience, accept Ms. Ireland's fifth answer. This decision gave her a final score of one out of five.

Tommy Lee or Gene Simmons?

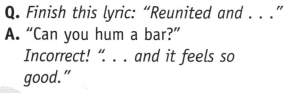

Bobcat Goldthwait

(score: 3/5)

Q. *Where is the best place to gawk at the Amish?*
A. "Ohhuhh I know this one, ahhh . . . Pennsylvania."
Correct!

Q. *Demonstrate the universal symbol for "Give me the check, please."*
A. "Uhhhhh . . . I've never picked up a check. Uh, what is it? Something with this?"
Incorrect! Can't accept that.

Q. *What do you call an omelet with green peppers, onions, and ham?*
A. "I would call that a, um, a colon bomb."
Incorrect! A western omelet, or a Denver omelet if you're very sophisticated.
"What kinda slam is that? 'Oh, I'm very continental, I've been to Denver.'"

Where is the best place to gawk at the Amish?

Q. *Finish this lyric:* *"Bye, bye, love . . ."*
A. *"'Bye, bye, happiness.'"*
Correct!

Q. *Are we tight?*
A. "Ah, yes, I would say we were tight. We're very tight. We're so tight, that you're willing to shake the hand that I just had under my armpit."
Correct!

Andy Dick

(score: 3/5)

Q. *What's the tallest building in North America?*
A. "The Hancock Building in Chicago."
Incorrect! Ooh, the Sears Tower in Chicago.

Q. *Who played Hymie the robot on the original* Get Smart?
A. "Don Adams."
Incorrect! Dick Gautier.
"Yes, I couldn't remember his name. You are making me look like an ass."
I think your suit did that itself.

Q. *How would you like that cooked?*
A. "Medium rare."
Correct!

How would you like that cooked?

Q. *Use the word "pugnacious" in a sentence.*
A. "Please don't be so pugnacious. Stubborn! I know that one."
Correct!

Q. *Do your best impersonation of Harry Carey.*
A. "What did he say, what was it? 'Holy cow!'"
Correct!

Wes Craven

(score: 5/6)

(Note: Wes has the unique distinction of being the first to answer "Brian Unger's Six Questions")

Q. *What is the capital of Ohio?*
A. "Columbus."
Correct!

Q. *Chainsaw: Craftsman or Black & Decker?*
A. "Black & Decker."
Correct!

Q. *Exactly where was the nightmare again?*
A. "On Elm Street."
Correct!

Q. *Finish this lyric: "I did the mash . . ."*
A. ". . . and shuttled your hash."
Incorrect! "I did the Monster Mash."

Q. *What is a Raisinet?*

A. *"A small razor."*
Correct! A small chocolate-covered raisin, but we'll accept a small or female raisin—or what you just said.

Q. *What scares you?*

A. *"Bad question; I don't have an answer for that."*
Correct!

Chainsaw:
Craftsman or
Black & Decker?

Connie Britton

(score: 2/5)

You studied Chinese, didn't you?
"Yes, but if you ask me any
Chinese questions I'm going to
be humiliated."

Q. *What's the capital of Taiwan?*
A. "Oh! I'm humiliated! Was that close?"
Taiwan . . .
"Taiwan . . . City."
Incorrect! Taipei.

*You're doing a movie right now with Jon Bon Jovi,
right?*
"Yes."

Q. *Besides "You Give Love a Bad Name," what is your
favorite Bon Jovi song?*
A. "Um, that one . . . wait, does he do the one about
somebody's got a gun?"
*Can we accept that for "Wanted, Dead or Alive?"
Incorrect! No, I'm sorry we can't accept that.*

Q. *What is the main ingredient of hummus?*
A. "Chickpeas."
Correct!

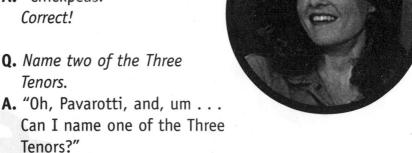

Q. *Name two of the Three Tenors.*
A. "Oh, Pavarotti, and, um . . . Can I name one of the Three Tenors?"
You just named the biggest one, can that count as two?
"He's very big."
Incorrect! Placido.

Q. *¿Donde está el baño?*
A. "Which way to the bathroom?"
Correct! We're gonna give that to you.

What's the capital of Taiwan?

Marilu Henner

(score: 3/5)

Q. *Location: That's the night the lights went out.*
A. "Georgia."
Correct!

Q. *What's the Badger State?*
A. "Indiana."
Incorrect! Wisconsin.

Q. *Name your favorite Neil Diamond song.*
A. "Ewwww. Um . . ."
Correct! None, which is where she was heading.

What was your birth weight?

Q. *What was your birth weight?*
A. "Seven-three."
Correct! Seven pounds, six ounces, but you always lie about your weight.

Q. *What is the technical term for the glob of whipped cream on pumpkin pie?*
A. "I'm a nondairy kind of girl; I won't even answer that question. I won't honor that question with an answer."
Incorrect! A dollop.

Betty White
(score: 4/5)

Q. *What is located at 1600 Pennsylvania Avenue?*
A. "The White House."
Correct!

Q. *More panache, Howie Mandel or Joe Piscopo?*
A. "Can I have another category? Um, Joe Piscopo?"
Incorrect! We're going with Howie Mandel, it's obvious.

Q. *What are the ingredients of Veal Prince Orloff?*
A. "Well you start with some veal, go out and get a prince, and then add some Orloff, too."
Correct!

Q. *Finish this lyric: "A little song, a little dance . . ."*

A. *"'A little seltzer down the pants.'"*
Correct!

Q. *Let's play a little password . . . "Farrah . . ."*

A. *"Khan, no, um . . . , tap, oh Fawcett!"*
Correct!

What are the ingredients of Veal Prince Orloff?

Kathy Kinney

(score: 3/5)

Q. *What are the team colors of the Packers?*
A. "Green and yellow."
Correct!

Q. *What is the difference between sherbert and sorbet?*
A. "Sherbet actually has dairy in it."
Correct!

Q. *With the exception of "Canary in a Coal Mine,"
name your favorite Police song.*
A. "'I Love You, My Friend the Cop'?"
Incorrect! "Roxanne."

What are the team colors of the Packers?

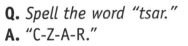

Q. *Spell the word "tsar."*
A. *"C-Z-A-R."*
   Incorrect! We were looking for T-S-A-R.

Q. *Are you the best you can be?*
A. *"Yes."*
   Correct!

Richard Dean Anderson

(score: 2/5)

Q. *Who turned the world on with her smile?*
A. "Is that Lizz?"
Incorrect! Mary Tyler Moore.

Q. *Name Emilio Estevez's costar in "Repo Man."*
A. "Would there be a Chuck Sheen in there?"
Incorrect! Harry Dean Stanton.

Q. *Name the secretary-general of the U.N.*
A. "Dean Stanton."
Incorrect! Boutros Boutros-Ghali.

Q. *Who's the blond woman who ruined Van Halen?*

A. "Which one? . . . Uh, oh! Is it . . . David Lee Roth?"
Correct!

Q. *Who was the midwestern serial killer who moonlighted as a clown?*

A. "John Wayne Gacy."
Correct!

Who was the Midwestern serial killer who moonlighted as a clown?

John Salley

(score: 4/5)

Q. *Name two of the Great Lakes.*
A. "Michigan and Erie."
Correct!

Q. *With the exception of Dadaism, what is your favorite art movement?*
A. No answer.
Incorrect!

Q. *What makes John Denver happy?*
A. "Weed."
Yeah, okay. Also, sunshine on my/his shoulder.

The Daily Show's Five Questions

With the exception of Dadaism, what is your favorite art movement?

Q. *Who dunks better, Jordan or Dr. J?*
A. "Dr. J."
Correct!

Q. *What is the ingredient that separates a Snickers from a Milky Way?*
A. "Nougat. Nuts."
Correct!

David Arquette
(score: 3/5)

Q. *Where is Yasgur's farm?*
A. "Oh, man, you're really hittin' me with it. Uh . . .
Portland."
*Incorrect! Ooh! We're goin' the other way. Bethel,
New York, also Woodstock.*

Q. *Who is best remembered for occupying the lower
left cubicle on* Hollywood Squares?
A. "My grandfather! Cliff Arquette, or better known as
Charlie Weaver."
Correct!

Q. *Favorite Chinese dish.*
A. "My favorite Chinese dish is sweet-and-sour chicken."
Incorrect! No, I'm sorry, it's actually tangerine beef.

Q. *Finish this song lyric: "Sugar sugar . . ."*

A. *"'Ah, honey honey. You are my candy girl . . .'"*
Correct!

Q. *Did your older sisters ever dress you up in their clothes when you were growing up?*

A. *"Actually, once Patricia did."*
Correct!

Who is best remembered for occupying the lower left cubicle on *Hollywood Squares?*

Peri Gilpin

(score: 4/5)

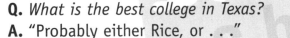

Q. *What is the best college in Texas?*
A. "Probably either Rice, or . . ."
Correct! "Rice, where my brother went."

Q. *How many ounces are in a pint?*
A. "Sixteen."
Correct!

Q. *Who starred in* Bill and Ted's Excellent Adventure?
A. "Keanu Reeves and oh . . . "
. . . and the other guy, correct!

What is the best college in Texas?

Q. *Better dessert: fresh fruit or hot apple cobbler?*
A. "Fresh fruit?"
Incorrect! No, hot apple cobbler, with vanilla ice cream.

Q. *Finally, Peri, did your dad want a boy, Peri?*
A. "They were expecting one."
Correct! We're gonna accept that.

Jamie Foxx

(score: 3/5)

Q. *What is the state bird of Texas?*
A. "There's not a state bird—oh, there is? It's the Kentucky Fried Chicken."
Incorrect! It's the mockingbird, but we would've accepted Lady Bird Johnson.

Q. *What's your favorite Barry Manilow song?*
A. "Copacabana."
Correct! "Copacabana" or "Mandy."

Q. *What's the best Pop Tart flavor?*
A. "Strawberry."
Incorrect! Brown Sugar Cinnamon.

Q. *Use the words "zestfully" and "clean" in a sentence.*
A. "I feel zestfully clean."
Correct!

Q. *Why is the sky blue?*
A. "The sky is blue because the sun reflects off of the ocean and the ocean is blue, therefore . . . "
Correct!

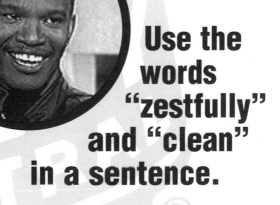

Use the words "zestfully" and "clean" in a sentence.

Maureen McCormick

(score 3/5)

Q. *You were in the play* Grease. *Where's the Acropolis?*
A. "Athens."
Correct!

Q. *What gun control law did President Clinton sign on November 25, 1993?*
A. "I have no idea."
Incorrect. The Brady bill.

Q. *Finish the Stylistics' song lyric. "You are everything . . ."*
A. ". . . and more."
Incorrect.

What the hell is Wessonality?

Q. *Sam the Butcher's sausage: Sweet or hot?*
A. "Hot!"
Correct!

Q. *What the hell is Wessonality?*
A. "It's really great."
Correct!

from Comedy Central

Suzanne Sommers

(score 2/5)

Q. *Where are the Spanish Steps?*
A. "Spain, I'm not stupid."
Right! (Actually, they're in Rome.)

Q. *Lemon Jell-O or Chocolate Pudding?*
A. "Jell-O."
Wrong!

Q. *Who's the slowest gun in the West?*
A. "Maverick."
No, sorry, Don Knotts.

Q. *Finish the Snoop Doggy Dog song lyric: "Bow Wow Wow . . ."*

A. "Get off my cow."
No!

Q. *You're an actress, so can you show me bemused resignation?*

A. (Gives the look.)
That's it!

Finish the Snoop Doggy Dog song lyric: "Bow Wow Wow . . ."

Rebecca Lobo

(score 4/5)

Q. *What is the longest river in Brazil?*
A. "Rio."
Incorrect! the Amazon.

Q. *Who sang "Me and You and a Dog Named Boo"?*
A. "Lobo."
Correct!

Q. *What movie starred Mariel Hemingway and Patrice Donnelly as a pair of Olympic athletes?*
A. "Personal Best."
Correct!

Who sang "Me and You and a Dog Named Boo"?

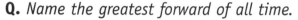

Q. *Name the greatest forward of all time.*
A. "Larry Bird."
Correct!

Q. *True or false: There may be one or two lesbians playing in the WNBA as we speak.*
A. "True."
Correct!

Debbie Reynolds

(score: 5/5)

Q. *What is the Lone Star State?*
A. "Texas."
Correct!

Q. *With the exception of lettuce and bacon bits, name two items found at a salad bar.*
A. "Beets, eggs chopped, mushrooms . . ."
Correct!

Q. *More attractive: Kevin Costner or a young Robert Wagner?*
A. "Well, I want them both!"
Correct!

Q. *On the weekends, who would you rather rock out to, Pearl Jam, Smashing Pumpkins, or Metallica?*

A. "Oh, I don't know, it sounds great to smash pumpkins, we could try that. Is that a real group?"
Correct!

Q. *Finish this sentence: "I'm dancing and . . ,"*

A. ". . . singing in the rain. Good morning!"
Correct!

More attractive: Kevin Costner or a young Robert Wagner?

Steve Guttenberg

(score: 2/5)

Q. *The first Bible printed on a press was . . .*
A. *". . . a book?"*
Incorrect! The Gutenberg.

Q. *Name a popular Hungarian stew.*
A. *"Roxanne!"*
Incorrect! Goulash.

Q. *Name a peanut cousin of the Raisinet.*
A. *"Oh, Goober!"*
Correct!

Name a peanut cousin of the Raisinet.

Q. *Who sang, "Too Shy Shy"?*
A. "The Goulets! The Goulet family!"
Incorrect! Kajagoogoo.

Q. *Can I call you Goot?*
A. "Yeah, man, that's what everyone calls me!"
Correct!

Montel Williams

(score: 3/5)

Q. *What is the state bird of Maryland?*
A. "Oriole."
Correct!

Q. *Name one of the seven wonders of the world.*
A. "It's amazing, it's Gordon Elliott's head."
Correct! That or Steve Guttenberg's career.

Q. *What plumps when you cook 'em?*
A. "In what oven are you talking about? Oh, it was a Pillsbury thing, the dough-boy guy."
Incorrect! Ballpark Franks.

Q. *Boxers or briefs?*
A. "Neither."
Incorrect! Either, but not neither.

Q. *Should teens go to jail for having sex?*
A. "The reason—it was on my September 9th show in 1996—is because there was a law passed in a state that put kids in jail for having sex, and I said, Absolutely not. But, when a girl underage has sex with a teen, he should go to jail."
Correct!

What plumps when you cook 'em?

David Allan Grier

(score: 3/5)

Q. *Where is the U.S. Naval Academy?*
A. "Annapolis."
Correct!

Q. *An analogy: Grape is to raisin as "blank" is to prune.*
A. "Plum."
Correct!

Q. *Finish this Dan Hill lyric: "Sometimes when we touch . . ."*
A. "'Our feet . . . uh, the smell of you is too much.' No, 'the feelings are much too much.' 'The thought of you is too much.'"
Incorrect! Close, ". . . the honesty is too much." Can't accept that.

Better career move, *Celebrity Jeopardy* or *Circus of the Stars?*

Q. *Better career move,* Celebrity Jeopardy *or* Circus of the Stars*?*
A. *"Circus of the Stars,* I gotta go with that."
Incorrect! No, Celebrity Jeopardy. *It's a cool show.*

Q. *Is it okay to use a toothpick at the table?*
A. "At my table it certainly is."
Correct! Yes, just cover your mouth.

Carol Alt

(score: 3/5)

Q. *What is the mail abbreviation for Michigan?*
A. *"M-I."*
   Correct!

Q. *What is the makeup that feels like no makeup?*
A. *"Dior."*
   Incorrect! Cover Girl.

Q. *How much niacin is in the average apple?*
A. *"50 milligrams."*
   Incorrect! 0.6 milligrams.

Is Fabio's head too big for his body?

Q. *Is Fabio's head too big for his body?*
A. "No, but his hair is too big for his head!"
Correct!

Q. *Why?*
A. "Nobody knows."
Correct!

from Comedy Central

Kenny Anderson

(score: 4/5)

Q. *What city is Puck from?*
A. "From the Bay area . . . San Francisco."
Correct!

Q. *Which fast-food chain sells square burgers with five holes and just the right amount of grease?*
A. "White Castle."
Correct!

Q. *Finish this Tony Orlando & Dawn lyric: "Knock three times . . ."*
A. "I know it's a song, but it's on the tip of my tongue, I can't . . . I don't know."
Incorrect! ". . . on the ceiling if you want me."

Q. *Late at night, do you ever find yourself thinking about Dennis Rodman?*
A. "Hell, no."
Correct!

Q. *Who's more fun on the road: Marv Albert or Frank Gifford?*
A. "Marv Albert."
Correct!

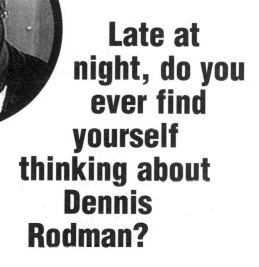

Late at night, do you ever find yourself thinking about Dennis Rodman?

Dr. Joyce Brothers

(score: 5/5)

Q. *Where was Sigmund Freud born?*
A. "In Vienna."
Correct!

Q. *More strapping: Hulk Hogan or Jesse "The Body" Ventura?*
A. "Oh, I worked with Hulk Hogan and he is strapping."
Correct!

Q. *The difference between brisket and pot roast?*
A. "It's a different part of the uh . . . um . . . steak."
Correct! Brisket is a cut of meat, pot roast is a method of cooking.

Use the phrase "pump up the jam" in a sentence.

Q. *Use the phrase "pump up the jam" in a sentence.*
A. "Well, I'm really tired, but I'm going to go to the gym and I'm going to 'pump up the jam.'"
Correct!

Q. *Is it bad that I like to be spanked?*
A. "It's wonderful for someone who loves to spank you."
Correct!

Sharon Lawrence

(score 4/5)

Q. *What is the Palmetto State?*
A. "South Carolina."
Correct!

Q. *Who plays the hostage in* Ruthless People?
A. "Bette Midler."
Correct!

Q. *What bologna has a first name?*
A. "Oscar Mayer."
Correct!

What bologna has a first name?

Q. *Better butt: David Caruso or Jimmy Smits?*
A. "I gotta go for Mr. Smits."
Incorrect!

Q. *Don't you think basic cable is the future of our industry?*
A. "It's probably your future."
Correct!

from Comedy Central

Timothy Dalton

(score: 3/5)

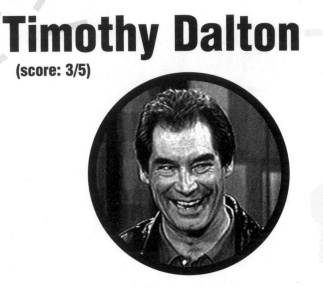

Q. *What is the capital of India?*
A. "I remember that. Delhi. Bombay."
Incorrect! New Delhi.

Q. *What's the difference between eggs Benedict and eggs Florentine?*
A. "Spinach."
Correct!

Q. *Finish this Wayne Newton lyric: "Danke schoen, darling . . ."*
A. "'Auf Weidersehen.'"
Incorrect! ". . . danke schoen."

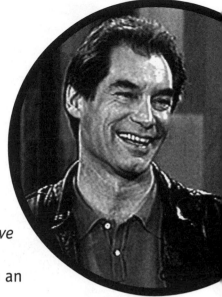

Q. *Shaken or stirred?*
A. "Not. Shaken, not stirred."
Correct!

Q. *Why don't British pop stars have accents when they sing?*
A. "Because they're appealing to an American audience."
Correct!

Why don't British pop stars have accents when they sing?

Belinda
Carlisle

(score: 4/5)

Q. *Where was the Hitchcock movie* To Catch a Thief *set?*
A. "The South of France."
Correct.

Q. *What is Yorkshire pudding usually served with?*
A. "Beef."
Prime rib. That's a tough one. Can't accept that.

What is
Yorkshire
pudding
usually
served with?

Q. *With the exception of "Walk Like an Egyptian,"
name your favorite Bangles song.*
A. "Bell Jar."
Yeah!

Q. *What do you miss most about America, swimming
off Malibu or affordable health care?*
A. "Swimming off Malibu."
Yes, Malibu!

Q. *Finally, say something in French.*
A. "Je t'aime."
Je t'aime! I love you! I love you!

Robin Leach

(score: 1/5)

Q. *What's the Buckeye State?*
A. "I'm an Englishman living in America!"
Incorrect! Ohio.

Q. *Ketchup: Heinz or Hunt's?*
A. "Heinz."
Correct! Hunt's is thirty cents less for a reason.

Q. *Name your favorite P. Funk All-Star.*
A. "Who the hell is P. Funk? . . . Ohio!"
Incorrect! Bootsie or George Clinton.

Q. *How long was the Gilligan's Island tour supposed to be?*
A. *"As tall as Ginger is—six and a half weeks."*
Incorrect! Three hours.

Q. *In a formal place setting, what utensil goes to the right of the soup spoon?*
A. *"The butter knife."*
Incorrect! The oyster fork.

Name your favorite P. Funk All-Star.

Andrew Dice Clay

(Score 3/5)

Q. *Where are the headquarters of the National Organization for Women?*
A. "In my guesthouse."
No!

Q. *Name your favorite Helen Reddy song.*
A. "There's only one . . . you know that one . . . the only one that people listen to."
Incorrect!

Q. *Funnier on stage: Howie Mandel or Carrot Top?*
A. "Howie Mandel."
Correct!

Where are the headquarters of the National Organization for Women?

Q. *Use the word "misogynist" in a sentence.*
A. "Andrew Dice Clay can sometimes be a little misogynistic."
Correct!

Q. *Dice, when was the last time you had a good cry?*
A. "Arsenio 1989."
Correct!

from Comedy Central

Matt Stone & Trey Parker

(score 5/5)

Q. *Name five of the seven states
that border Colorado.*

A. "Arizona, New Mexico, Utah, Oklahoma, Kansas."
All right!

Q. *What was the first X-rated cartoon?*

A. "Fritz The Cat."
Yes!

Q. *Rob and Fab were the frontmen for what group?*

A. "Milli Vanilli."
Yes!

What was the first X-rated cartoon?

Q. *Christmas: Celebrating the birth of Jesus or grabbing the goodies from Santa?*
A. "Birth of Jesus."
Correct!

Q. *Do you have to hang out with George Clooney?*
A. "His day is done. No more."
Correct!

Adam Arkin

(Score 3/5)

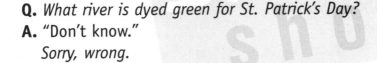

Q. *What river is dyed green for St. Patrick's Day?*
A. "Don't know."
Sorry, wrong.

Q. *What is your favorite Nancy Dusseault film?*
A. "You're mean. These are hard."
Sorry!

Q. *Was George Clooney a very bad Batman?*
A. "No, he was a good Batman."
All right. You're a nice guy.

Q. *Finish this lyric: Doctor, my eyes have seen the years . . .*
A. "And the slow parade of tears."
Yes, all right!

Q. *Turn my head and cough: What am I going to do?*
A. "Grab something."
Yes!

Turn my head and cough: What am I going to do?

Jerry Springer

(score: 3/5)

Q. *What is the Beaver State?*
A. "Oregon."
Correct!

Q. *What is a fricassee?*
A. "A salad."
Incorrect! Meat, usually chicken, stewed and served with a white sauce.

Q. *Name the Rose Marie character from* The Dick Van Dyke Show.
A. (No response.)
Incorrect! Sally Rogers.

Who wins in a cage match, Geraldo Rivera or Gordon Elliott?

Q. *Who wins in a cage match, Geraldo Rivera or Gordon Elliott?*
A. "Geraldo."
Correct!

Q. *Finish this sentence: "My mother made me . . ."*
A. ". . . clean my room?"
Correct!

from Comedy Central

Denis Leary
(score 2/5)

Q. *Which New York area airport allows smoking?*
A. "Lock and load."
No!

Q. *What's in a "Black and Tan"?*
A. "Half Guinness, half Harps."
Yes!

Q. *Better athletes: Hockey or hoops?*
A. "Hockey."
No.

Who is the best-looking actor today?

Q. *Who is the best-looking actor today?*
A. "Me."
Yes!

Q. *You're a cow. Point to where a sirloin steak would come from.*
A. "The crotch."
No!

Richard Belzer

(score 4/5)

Q. *Ou est la toilet?*
A. "Where's the bathroom?"
Yeah!

Q. *More tempting dessert: Fudge brownie or crème brûlée?*
A. "Crème brûlée."
Yes.

Q. *What is the new team name for the Washington Bullets?*
A. "The Wizards."
Yes!

Q. *Name your least favorite Barry Levinson film?*

A. "I can't, I want to keep my job."
Oh, well. Incorrect.

Q. *In ten words or less, explain the Mickey Rourke thing.*

A. "The French love Jerry Lewis. Hit Mickey on the head with a bat and he's Jerry!"
Yes, right!

More tempting dessert: Fudge brownie or crème brûlée?

Pauly Shore

(score: 3/5)

Q. *Geography: Where is the man from?*
A. "Oh, the man happens to be from the universe!"
Incorrect! Encino.

Q. *What are the ingredients of a Fluffernutter?*
A. "Pecans, nutmeg, and Turbo-lawski."
Incorrect! Bread, Marshmallow Fluff, and peanut butter.

Q. *What is the last book you read?*
A. "The Diary of Anne Frank."
Correct!

What's wrong with kids today?

Q. *More attractive: Sandy Duncan or Valerie Harper?*
A. "Sandy Duncan."
Correct!

Q. *What's wrong with kids today?*
A. "Nothing."
Correct!

Jennifer Tilly

(score: 2/5)

Q. *Name the capital of Nevada.*
A. "Nevada."
Incorrect! Carson City.

Q. *What is in a "fuzzy navel"?*
A. "Fuzzy."
Incorrect! Peach Schnapps and orange juice.

Q. *Who starred in the original* Born Yesterday?
A. "Judy Holliday."
Correct!

The Daily Show's Five Questions

Tattoo
or
body
piercing?

Q. *Tattoo or body piercing?*
A. "I like tattoos but I think navel rings are awfully attractive also. I have none—I have pierced ears."
Incorrect! Neither—why would you want to do that to yourself?

Q. *Biggest turnoff?*
A. "Guys who ask me five questions that I'm not prepared for."
Correct!

from Comedy Central

Jim Breuer

(score: 2/5)

Q. *What's the capital of Peru?*
A. "Goat."
Incorrect! It's Lima.

Q. *With the exception of the Amish beard sans the moustache, what's the most irritating facial hair?*
A. "The wart hair."
Incorrect! The "soul patch" on the chin.

Q. *Name the Pat Morita character in* The Karate Kid.
A. "Goat."
Incorrect! Mr. Miyagi.

With the exception of the Amish beard sans the moustache, what's the most irritating facial hair?

Q. *An extra-dry martini contains:*
   a) very little gin
   b) very little vermouth
   c) equal parts gin and vermouth
A. "Very little vermouth."
   Correct!

Q. *Why are Band-Aids so hard to open?*
A. "It's because of the goat."
   Correct!

Rita Rudner

(score: 2/5)

Q. *Where . . .*
A. *"Philadelphia!"*
  . . .were you born?"
  "Miami!"
  Correct! We'll accept that.

Q. *What's the difference between a model and a supermodel?*
A. *"Um, pigtails."*
  Incorrect! They all look fine. I don't know the difference.

Q. *What was General Tso's favorite dish?*
A. *"Fish sticks."*
  Incorrect! Looking for chicken.

Know what? You're struggling right now. Here's an easy one.

Q. *In what year did King John issue the Magna Carta?*
A. "1112."
Incorrect! You were within 100, 1215.

Q. *Use "hammertoe" in a sentence.*
A. "I hammered your toe."
Correct! We gotta give it to her, she is struggling.

Use "hammertoe" in a sentence.

Kurt Loder

(score: 2/5)

Q. *Name two Gibb brothers, excluding Andy.*
A. "Maurice and . . ."
We'll give that to you. Maurice and Robin.

Q. *Whose signature song is "If Ever I Would Leave You"?*
A. ". . . it would be in the summer? I don't know."
Incorrect! Robert Goulet.

Q. *By what name is Robert Van Winkle better known?*
A. "I forget, I don't know."
Incorrect! Vanilla Ice.

Name both of Gilbert O'Sullivan's hits.

Q. *Name both of Gilbert O'Sullivan's hits.*
A. "Oh, stop! That's not fair!"
Incorrect! "Claire" and "Alone Again Naturally."

Q. *How do you like your women, softly toned or skin and bones?*
A. "The better part of the two combined."
Okay—we're going to take that. It's neither—it's what's inside that counts.

Kim Coles

(score: 3/5)

Q. *Where is Old Faithful?*
A. "Yellowstone Park."
Correct!

Q. *Would you like fresh ground pepper on that?*
A. "Yes, I would, thank you."
Correct!

Q. *Name at least one nonmagnetic metal.*
A. "Iron!"
Incorrect! Ooh, there's so many here and that's not one of them.

Q. *You're on the green, what club are you going to use?*

A. "A club sandwich."
Incorrect! Can't accept that.

Q. *Finally . . . am I really all that?*

A. "You're all . . . as we say, you're all that *and* a bag of chips."
Correct!

Finally . . . am I really all that?

ACKNOWLEDGMENTS

Many people have helped in putting this pseudo-seminal work into print, and their yeoman efforts will not go unacknowledged. Therefore, here are the acknowledgements:

Thanks to *Daily Show* executive producer Madeleine Smithberg for reminding me that "Five Questions" is wrong in a bar but right on our show. I think of Madeleine as simply the best producer in the business.

Thanks to Comedy Central president Doug Herzog and senior vice president Eileen Katz for actually giving me a show.

Thanks to *Daily Show* studio producer Hank Gallo for actually getting these celebrities to appear on the show.

Thanks to Kate Post for helping Hank in his quest (his begging) to get these celebrities to appear on the show.

Thanks to my Comedy Central colleagues Frank Quinn, Vinny Sainato, and Larry Lieberman for doing whatever it is that they do best—and as soon as I know what that is I'll write another book.

And, finally, thanks to you, my adoring fans—you're so patient.

Love to all,
Craiggers